REMARKABLE PEOPLE

Justin Timberlake

by James De Medeiros

Published by Weigl Publishers Inc.
350 5th Avenue, Suite 3304, PMB 6G
New York, NY 10118-0069

Website: www.weigl.com

Library of Congress Cataloging-in-Publication Data

De Medeiros, James.
 Justin Timberlake / James De Medeiros.
   p. cm. -- (Remarkable people)
 Includes index.
 ISBN 978-1-59036-982-1 (hard cover : alk. paper) -- 978-1-59036-983-8 (soft cover
: alk. paper)
 1. Timberlake, Justin, 1981---Juvenile literature. 2. Singers--United States--
Biography--Juvenile literature. 1. Title.
 ML3930.T58 D4 2009
 782.42164092--b22
 [B]
                             2008003964

Printed in the United States of America
1 2 3 4 5 6 7 8 9 0 12 11 10 09 08

Editor: Danielle LeClair
Design: Terry Paulhus

Photograph Credits

Weigl acknowledges Getty Images as the primary image supplier for this title.
Unless otherwise noted, all images herein were obtained from Getty Images and
its contributors.

Other photograph credits include: Corbis: page 4 (background); Dreamstime: page
13 (bottom).

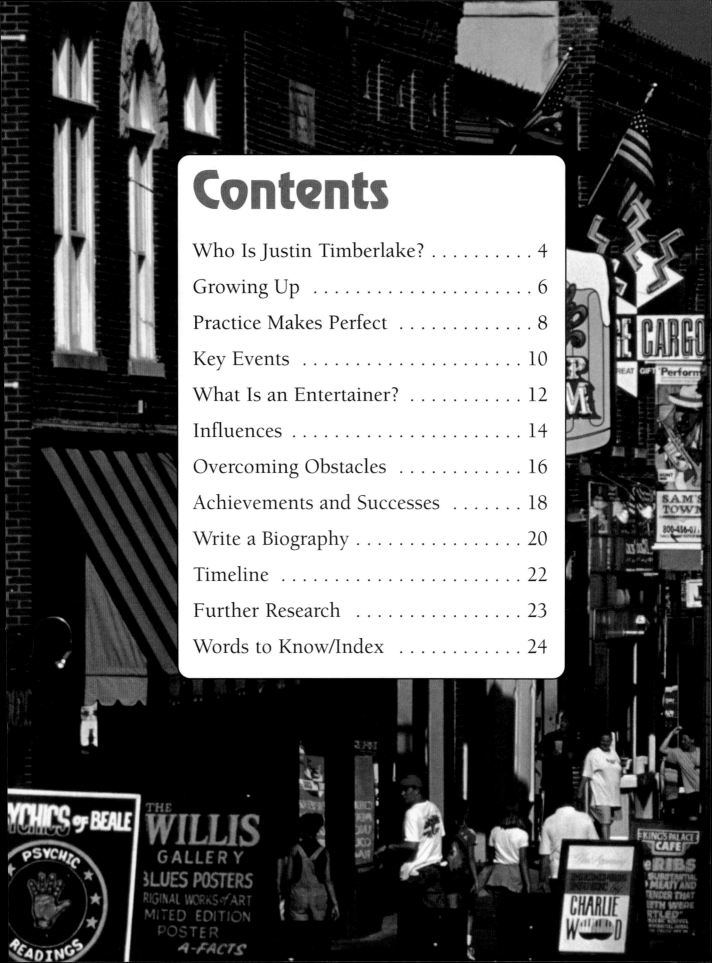

Contents

Who Is Justin Timberlake?

Justin Timberlake is an entertainer and **executive**. He is a singer, dancer, actor, songwriter, and businessman. Since he was a young boy, Justin has loved performing. He always dreamed of being an entertainer and sharing his love of music with others. Justin's career began when he was 11 years old. By the time he was 14, Justin was singing, dancing, recording music, and touring the world. In 2002, Justin released a **solo album**. He quickly earned a *Billboard* hit with his song "Like I Love You." For more than 16 years, Justin has worked hard to make his dreams come true, and his work has paid off. His abilities as an entertainer have allowed Justin to follow his other dreams. He has started his own record label, opened a restaurant, and has created a popular line of clothing. Justin is one of the most well-known and recognizable people in the world.

> "If you put out 150 percent, then you can always expect 100 percent back. That's what I was always told as a kid, and it's worked for me so far!"

Growing Up

Justin Randall Timberlake was born on January 31, 1981, in Memphis, Tennessee. He grew up in a small town in Tennessee called Millington. Justin's parents divorced when he was very young. Then, when he was five years old, his mother remarried. Justin was raised by his mother, Lynn, and his step-father, Paul Harless.

Justin's birth father, Randall, was a singer and **choir** director at a **Baptist** church in Millington. As he was growing up, Justin sang in church. Singing, and listening to the soulful voices of gospel singers, encouraged Justin's love of music and performing.

Even as a baby, Justin would dance to the **rhythm** of music. By the time he was two, he was singing and performing for his family. Justin's family noticed his interest in music, so his grandfather taught him to play guitar.

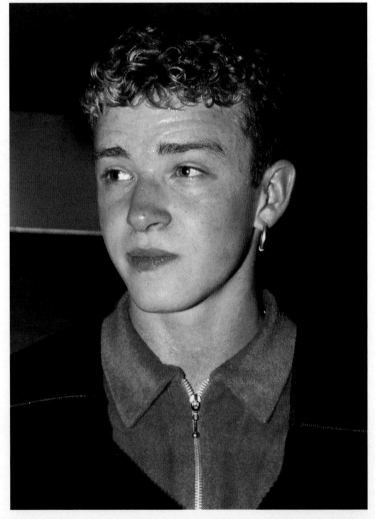

■ With his head of tight curls, Justin's family called him "Curly."

Get to Know Tennessee

ANIMAL
Raccoon

FLAG

FLOWER
Iris

Memphis was the home of Elvis Presley, the king of rock and roll.

Singer Aretha Franklin, known as the "Queen of Soul," was born in Memphis.

Memphis is known as the home of blues music.

The official song of Tennessee is "Rocky Top."

The square dance is the official dance of Tennessee.

Think about it!

When Justin was 11 years old, he moved to Orlando, Florida, to pursue his entertainment career. For six months each year, Justin lived away from his home in Tennessee. Imagine living away your family and your friends. If you lived away from home, what would you have to leave behind? What would you take with you to make you more at home in your new place?

Practice Makes Perfect

As Justin grew, so did his love of singing and dancing. By the time he was eight years old, Justin had a singing coach. His name was Bob Westbrook. Bob taught Justin how to use his voice like an instrument. As Justin worked hard and continued to improve, Bob and Lynn, Justin's mother, began to enter him in singing contests. When he was 10 years old, Justin sang at a **charity** evening at the **Grand Ole Opry**.

After performing in many local shows, Justin **auditioned** to compete in the junior vocalist category on the national television show *Star Search*. The winner received $25,000.00. Though thousands of children auditioned, *Star Search* was looking for two children to compete, and Justin won a spot. His singing impressed the audience and the judges, but Justin lost the contest.

■ Justin was the lead songwriter on the most recent *N SYNC album, called *Celebrity*.

When *Star Search* ended, Justin's mother heard that auditions were being held for *The Mickey Mouse Club*. Justin went to the audition and did well. The producers asked him to come back to perform for them again. Justin was graded on his appearance, personality, comfort in front of the camera, and dancing and acting abilities. His grades in each category were high, and he won a role on the show.

Justin spent two years singing, dancing, and acting on *The Mickey Mouse Club*. When the show ended, he was asked to join a new all-male singing group. The group, called *N SYNC, had five members, and Justin was the youngest. He was just 15 years old. *N SYNC moved to Germany to rehearse their songs and dance routines. In 1998, the band returned to the United States to perform in a Disney channel concert. After the concert, sales of their first CD, called *N SYNC, soared.

■ Justin does not allow alcohol or cigarettes in the backstage area during a concert. He wants the people he performs with, and the environment, to be healthy.

Key Events

After seven years of singing and performing around the world, Justin and the other members of *N SYNC decided to take a break. In 2002, Justin released a solo album called *Justified*. The songs on the album were different from the songs *N SYNC sang. Justin hoped people would appreciate his songs and take him seriously as a musician. He was nervous about releasing his own album.

That year, *Justified* was nominated for five Grammy awards. Justin won the Grammy awards for Best Pop Vocal Album and Best Male Pop Vocal Performance for the song "Cry Me a River."

During the years after *Justified* became a success, Justin began to make his other dreams come true. In 2005, he made his film debut in a movie, *Edison*. Then, in 2007, Justin started his own record label, called Tennman Records. He also opened a restaraunt in New York city, with his best friend, Trace, called "Southern Hospitality."

■ Justin grew up listening to many types of music, including rhythm and blues, rock and roll, country, and gospel music. They helped shape Justin's musical style.

Thoughts from Justin

Justin has always loved performing. Here are some things he has said about his life and his love of being an entertainer.

Justin appreciates his family.

"I have really great, great parents, and they were very supportive of me."

Justin understands the music history of Memphis, Tennessee.

"Historically, the city's been a melting pot for all kinds of music. It's the home of Elvis but also of B.B. King. You've got rock and blues, but Nashville's right down the road."

Justin is influenced by music in Tennessee.

"The many sounds of Memphis shaped my early musical career and continue to be an inspiration to this day."

Justin wants to do more acting and fewer concerts in the future.

"Ten years from now, I don't want to be jumping around on stage."

Justin loves the chance to be creative in any field.

"The reason I got into film is because I needed something inspiring, but more intimate, that I didn't have to do in front of 18,000 people every night."

Justin appreciates his fans.

"The fans have been great to me. I don't think it's asking too much to have me sign something for them."

What Is an Entertainer?

An entertainer is a person who uses his or her creative abilities to please or amuse others. Entertainers sing, dance, act, do stand-up comedy, and write. Some entertainers can do many of these things well, like Justin. Others focus or **specialize** in one area. Entertainers appear in events and performances, such as stage, cabarets, comedy shows, circuses, and street theatre. Most of their work is performed for live audiences.

In addition to performing, entertainers go to auditions and rehearsals. Beginners develop their skills by learning everything they can and practicing every day. It may take years of coaching, practice, and dedication to fully develop their skills. While some entertainers become famous, many performers work and entertain people around the world without becoming as recognizable as Justin.

■ Justin has always enjoyed dancing, although he has never taken any professional dance lessons.

Entertainers 101

Donnie Wahlberg (1969–)

Achievements: Singer, songwriter, producer, and actor

Donnie Wahlberg grew up in Dorchester, Massachusetts. When he was 15 years old, Donnie became a member of a group called New Kids on the Block. The band was very popular in the late 1980s. Donnie made his acting debut in the 1996 movie *Bullet*. He also has made appearances on television shows. Donnie has written songs for movies such as *The Mighty Ducks* and *Super Mario Bros*. Donnie's younger brother is singer and actor Mark Wahlberg.

Jennifer Love Hewitt (1979–)

Achievements: Actress, singer, songwriter, and producer

Jennifer Love Hewitt began appearing in television commercials at the age of 10. When she was 11 years old, Jennifer appeared on the television show *Kids Incorporated*. As a singer, Jennifer released four albums between 1992 and 2002. In 1995, Jennifer earned her first starring role in the television show *Party of Five*. Then, in 2005, she returned to television with a starring role in the show *Ghost Whisperer*. Jennifer has starred in more than 20 movies.

Jessica Simpson (1980–)

Achievements: Singer and actress

Jessica Simpson released her first single, "I Wanna Love You Forever," in 1999. It became a *Billboard* top 10 hit. Soon, she began releasing albums and touring with the band 98 Degrees. In 2002, Jessica married Nick Lachey, a member of 98 Degrees. Nick and Jessica had a popular reality show called *Newlyweds: Nick and Jessica*. Then, in 2005, Jessica starred in her first movie, *Dukes of Hazzard*. She is the International Ambassador for "Operation Smile," which provides health care treatment for children and young adults.

Hillary Duff (1987–)

Achievements: Singer and actress

Hillary started her career appearing in commercials. She had her first of many starring roles in the 1998 movie *Casper Meets Wendy*. In 2001, Hillary became the star of the Disney show *Lizzie McGuire*. The show gave her the opportunity to sing. Since that time, Hillary has produced hit albums, including "Metamorphosis," "Hillary Duff," and "Dignity." Hillary devotes part of her time to charity. She helped Hurricane Katrina victims and works with the charity Kids With a Cause.

Billboard Charts

The *Billboard* charts are found in *Billboard* magazine. The charts ranks a song's popularity. The more popular the song is, the lower the *Billboard* number. Every singer hopes to have a number one song on the *Billboard* charts. A song's popularity is judged by the number of times it is played on the radio, as well as the number of copies it sells.

Influences

Justin's family, his teachers, and other entertainers have been an influence in his life. Justin's family has always been supportive and encouraging of his dreams. His grandfather, Charles L. Timberlake, was a Baptist minister who taught him to play an instrument. Justin's father was a choir director and encouraged Justin to sing at church. Though Justin is known for his singing and dancing, many people believe part of what makes him such a good entertainer is his personal style. Justin gets his sense of style from his step-father, who also taught him the importance of having a loving family.

Justin's mother, Lynn, has been his biggest supporter and fan. She saw potential in Justin and found teachers and coaches to help him achieve his dream.

■ Justin sang with legendary rock and roll singer James Brown at a concert to raise money for victims of the Asian tsunami disaster in 2005.

Justin's seventh grade teacher, Ms. Earnest, recognized Justin's talent and encouraged his acting and singing. She continues to work with Justin as a part of his management team.

Justin's favorite singers and entertainers include Elvis Presley, the Beach Boys, Michael Jackson, and Madonna. All of these entertainers have excellent voices and are outstanding entertainers. They had the ability to sing, write songs, act, and dance. Justin learned the importance of being a well-rounded entertainer from their examples.

THE TIMBERLAKE FAMILY

After his parents divorced, both Justin's mother and father remarried. Justin's mother, Lynn, and his step-father, Paul, did not have more children, so Justin was raised as an only child. Justin is very close to his mother. She travels with him and often joins Justin at awards ceremonies and movie premieres. Lynn is an entertainment manager. She runs a company that represents musicians, called "Justin-Time." Justin is also close to his step-father Paul. When Justin talks about Paul he remembers how patient and kind his step-father is. In fact, Justin has said that Paul is probably the greatest man he has ever known.

Justin is very close to his mother and step-father. He says that his mom is his best friend and that he tells her everything.

Overcoming Obstacles

Being famous is not easy for Justin. He has had to face many challenges. Even as a child, each time Justin would perform, he felt as though it was a test. Sometimes, people liked his performances. Other times, they did not. Justin had to listen to **criticism** and accept some failures. This was not easy, and it always hurt.

Justin's personal life is often difficult. As a celebrity, Justin receives a great deal of attention. Everywhere he goes, photographers and journalists follow. Radio, television, and newspapers report on every detail about his life, including where he goes, what he says, how he dressess, and how he behaves. Some of the reporting is not true. Justin has to deal with the stress of always being watched and criticized.

■ Though Justin is always ready to sign autographs for his fans, he says he is very shy and has a hard time talking to people he does not know.

One of the biggest obstacles Justin has had to overcome was when doctors discovered that he had throat nodules. These are unusual growths that develop on the vocal chords, and are painful. The problem is more common among singers, as singing puts a great deal of pressure and stress on their vocal cords. In 2005, Justin had to have surgery to remove the nodules.

Following the surgery, Justin was told not to sing or talk loudly for at least three months. While waiting for his vocal cords to heal, Justin did some acting. He was able to return to singing soon after. With his voice back to normal, Justin has recorded more number-one hit singles.

■ In 2007, Justin was the voice of Artie in *Shrek the Third*. That year, he also had a starring role in the film *Black Snake Moan* with Samuel L. Jackson.

Achievements and Successes

As an entertainer, Justin has won many awards. When Justin was with *N SYNC, the group set a one-week sales record with their album *No Strings Attached*. Later, as a solo singer, Justin won Grammy awards, Teen Choice awards, MTV Music awards, and American Music awards. In 2006, Justin's second solo album produced six top 20 *Billboard* hits. He was the first male recording artist to do this since Michael Jackson had with the album *Dangerous* in 1992.

In 2007, Justin and his best friend, Trace Ayala, created a line of clothing, called "William Rast." The company gets its name from Justin's grandfather's first name and Trace's grandfather's last name. Justin says they design clothes they think represent young people today.

■ As of 2008, Justin has been nominated for 24 Grammy awards and has won eight.

Justin's success has inspired him to help others. In 2001, with the help of the Giving Back Fund, Justin founded the Justin Timberlake Foundation to promote music education. The foundation believes that learning music helps children reach their full potential.

Justin works with other charities as well. In 2006, he helped the survivors of Hurricane Katrina by donating money from the sales of his songs through the iTunes Music Store. Then, in 2008, he agreed to host a Professional Golfers' Association (PGA) Tour. The profits from the tour were donated to the Shriners Hospital for Children. Justin also dedicates his time and money to other charities, including Mercy Corps, Mission Australia, MusiCares, Oxfam, and Wildlife Warriors Worldwide.

GIVING BACK

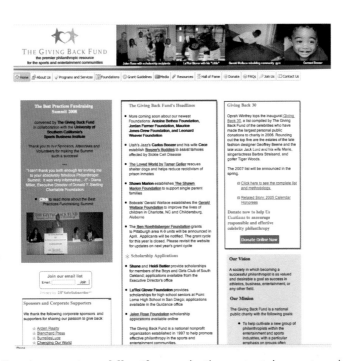

The Giving Back Fund promotes **philanthropy** in the entertainment and sports fields. It helps celebrities, including Justin, set up charitable organizations. The Giving Back Fund was founded in 1997. It has helped many entertainers and athletes create charities and foundations. Visit the Giving Back Fund at **www.givingback.org**.

Write a Biography

A person's life story can be the subject of a book. This kind of book is called a biography. Biographies describe the lives of remarkable people, such as those who have achieved great success or have done important things to help others. These people may be alive today, or they may have lived many years ago. Reading a biography can help you learn more about a remarkable person.

At school, you might be asked to write a biography. First, decide who you want to write about. You can choose an entertainer, such as Justin Timberlake, or any other person you find interesting. Then, find out if your library has any books about this person. Learn as much as you can about him or her. Write down the key events in this person's life. What was this person's childhood like? What has he or she accomplished? What are his or her goals? What makes this person special or unusual?

A concept web is a useful research tool. Read the questions in the following concept web. Answer the questions in your notebook. Your answers will help you write your biography review.

- Where does this individual currently reside?
- Does he or she have a family?

- What did you learn from the books you read in your research?
- Would you suggest these books to others?
- Was anything missing from these books?

- Where and when was this person born?
- Describe his or her parents, siblings, and friends.
- Did this person grow up in unusual circumstances?

Your Opinion

Adulthood

Childhood

WRITING A BIOGRAPHY

Main Accomplishments

Help and Obstacles

Work and Preparation

- What is this person's life's work?
- Has he or she received awards or recognition for accomplishments?
- How have this person's accomplishments served others?

- What was this person's education?
- What was his or her work experience?
- How does this person work; what is or was the process he or she uses or used?

- Did this individual have a positive attitude?
- Did he or she receive help from others?
- Did this person have a mentor?
- Did this person face any hardships?
- If so, how were the hardships overcome?

Timeline

YEAR	JUSTIN TIMBERLAKE	WORLD EVENTS
1981	Justin Timberlake is born on January 31, 1981.	MTV makes its debut on television playing music videos.
1992	Justin makes his national television debut on *Star Search*.	Country singer Johnny Cash is inducted into the Rock and Roll Hall of Fame.
1993	Justin joins *The Mickey Mouse Club* television show.	Country singer Garth Brooks tops the *Billboard* Year-End Charts as the Top Pop Artist of 1993.
1998	On March 24, *N SYNC releases its debut album, called *N SYNC*.	Music legend Frank Sinatra dies at the age of 82.
2002	Justin releases his first solo song, "Like I Love You." It reaches number 11 on the *Billboard* chart.	"A Little Less Conversation" by Elvis Presley is remixed and becomes a number one hit in more than 20 countries.
2005	Justin has his first starring movie role in *Edison*.	Top performers from around the world join together for the Asian tsunami disaster relief concerts.
2007	Justin creates his own record label, with Interscope Records company, called Tennman Records.	The worldwide concert Live Earth is held to raise awareness of climate change.

Further Research

How can I find out more about Justin Timberlake?

Most libraries have computers that connect to a database that contains information on books and articles about different subjects. You can input a key word and find material on that person, place, or thing you want to learn more about. The computer will provide you with a list of books in the library that contain information on the subject you searched for. Non-fiction books are arranged numerically, using their call number. Fiction books are organized alphabetically by the author's last name.

Websites

Find out more about Justin Timberlake at
www.justintimberlake.com

To see Justin's clothing line, visit
www.williamrast.com

Learn more about Justin's record company at
www.tennmanrecords.com

Words to Know

album: a collection of songs released in one package, such as a CD

auditioned: tried out for a part

Baptist: a Christian religion

charity: a group or organization that helps people in need

choir: an organized group of singers

criticism: pointing out the problems or mistakes in something

executive: the person responsible for managing and directing a company or organization

Grand Ole Opry: a weekly country music radio and television program broadcast live from Nashville, Tennessee

philanthropy: doing something for the better of humankind through donations or charity

rhythm: a pattern found in music

solo: to be the featured performer

specialize: to concentrate and become an expert on a particular subject

Index